SMALL ASCENSIONS

SMALL ASCENSIONS

Poems by William R. Soldan

SOUTHERNMOST BOOKS

Saint Augustine, FL 2022

For more information:
SouthernmostJournal@gmail.com

Published by Southernmost Books
Saint Augustine, FL

First Edition
ISBN: 9798218040833

Cover and interior design: Gavin Stephen Lambert III and William R. Soldan

Cover art: Tony Nicholas

Acknowledgements

I would like to thank the editors of the following publications, in which some of these poems first appeared, sometimes under different titles or in slightly different form:

Anti-Heroin Chic: "Poor Kid's Obituary"; "Eulogy"; and "Like Any Other"
Bending Genres: "On the Run, Returning"
Cholla Needles: "Dear Nostalgia"; "Poem Written in the Infirmary of the Old Mansfield Pen"; "Genovese" (under the title "Psych 101"); "Grand Plans"; "Gravities"; "13 Years" (under the title "13 Years, or Poem for My Wife Who Doesn't Really Do Poetry"); and "Springtime in Rip City"
Cloves Literary: "In Dreams"
Collapsed Lexicon: "Hopscotching Across this Rock"
Elm Leaves Journal: Blues Edition: "For Love"
Eunoia Review: "Notes on the Irretrievable Dream"; "Dream Poem: Taos, NM"; and "Mama"
Junkyard Kool: "The First Time She Died"
Live Nude Poems: "The Night I Left Work with a Pocketful of Cash on Fire"
Night Music Journal: "An Armor"
Ohio's Best Emerging Poets Anthology: "Death in the Courtyard of the House Where Dennis Hopper Lived," (2018) and "Swing Shifts and Doubles" (2017)
Punk Noir: "Poem for the Going and Gone"; "Before the Mind and Body Fail, as Is Their Fate"; "Winter Wedding at the VFW"; and "Come a Long Way" (under the title "How Far From")
The Raw Alternative: "Reunion: Cleveland, OH" and "Residual"
Rue Scribe: "Dust & Ash"
Sienna Heights Eclipse: "Ode: In Utero"
Volney Road Review: "Shoveling Snow"

I would also like to extend my deepest gratitude to all the people who have had a role in this book's creation, whether by reading early drafts of the pieces within, providing blurbs or epigraphs, or being among the very flesh and blood smeared across its pages, folks who shared in its lived experience.

To Steven Reese, Mindi Kirchner, Mary Biddinger, Robert Vaughan, Meg Tuite, and Len Kuntz. To HLR, Gabriel Hart, James Diaz, and Nick Gardner. To Alex DiFrancesco, Al Kratz, Jonathan Cardew, and Wilson Koewing. Sean Thomas Dougherty, Wislawa Szymborska, Jim Carroll, Jim Harrison, Philip Larkin, Denis Johnson, Octavio Paz, and Richard Lange. To Jessica Lynne, Victor Masters, Marcus Gutierrez, and Patrick Noon. To Tony Nicholas, fellow artist and friend, for his stunning cover photograph. Cheers, brother. Thanks for coming through. To my mother and the rest of my family, particularly my wife Rebecca and our two hellraisers, Spencer and Esmé. Y'all are my world, in this life and the rest. And to the readers and writers who've remained in my corner over the years, despite which genre I choose. Thank you. Much Love.

CONTENTS

1: Gravities

2: For Love

3: Somewhere Else

4: Minutiae

5: Of the Season

Notes

About the Author

For Rebecca, always

For those that made it

those that didn't

and the last of the lost

ones

1: Gravities

Let them gawk and ponder. We have no map to offer. To travel our weeping labyrinths.

—Sean Thomas Dougherty

a halottak nyelve

Beating in the cage of my estranged father's chest are the remains of our history, flickering faint and fading. The story of our blood, told low, hushed and near forgotten. Ours is a cartography of ruin, a vacancy strewn with all things broken—hearts and homes. Promises, to resuscitate a name, placed with shaking hands like flowers on the graves of our departed. But can we bring back a past unknown, a language set to be disassembled, undone? The language of a Hungarian rabbit farmer, crossing the ocean toward shores of more. Having it ripped from his throat, his tongue, stolen, the loss of it looming, its blooming negated. The language of wilting, of breaking, of making do. Becoming something else. The constant mining of a new continent, for the consonants and vowels to allow the right words. So this now is our new language, a slurry of sound and blur. Of search engines and bad translations. The insistent ring of a whirling world. A twisted linguistics. Language of branching birches, of cranes in flight like winged arrows piercing the heart of the sky. Of the wind in the grass, the distant drone of gunked-up motors winding out, of the rain Morse coding the undecipherable mantra of the clouds. Language of birds, their dizzying calligraphy. Of flies buzzing, of bombs, falling like acorns, budding like orchids sown in flames. A wound, too, is a language. A womb. A tomb. An exhumation. The language of orphans, shaping themselves into the names they've been given, of their songs, sung in grunts, the minor keys and hopeless tones of lonely. Language of their dead, graffitied across bricks and bus stop benches, slung on phone lines, the language of sneakers casting shadows on the street, on the blood that was left behind to dry brown in the sun. Language of sirens, catastrophe, of cost and bills come due. Of coins in pockets and placed over the eyes of those who've crossed over, of cash hissing between hands, of lampposts lending their lurid light, of pawnshop gates ratcheting upward. Language of the smell of memory. Of the votives lit, placed on the alter of our altered lineage, our inheritance, a blank page, a scattering of ghosts.

Dear Nostalgia,

So often I want to blame it all on God. But much of the past has been redacted. So much revised, a dozen days stitched into a single story. Such vast minutiae, the raining recollections, the accumulation of years. The gravel in the lot behind the hardware store. The short-lived lives of lilacs. The clink of coins too small to earn their wish. So many towns in which we'd stop and say, *This is where it will all turn around.* In search of a silver lining shining through the fog until time unraveled and the strands lay strewn, jagged as rivers across the map of us. These sloped streets strain to hold it all up. And how strange we remember one above another: The sun setting on the last pitch of a summer game but not the rock that drew blood. The sickroom glow rather than the sparrow preening on the fence. Even a child will someday learn the lie behind *That which doesn't kill us makes us stronger.* More likely it leaves us maimed and unstable. We speak so many ceaseless words, and the nights are so rarely clear membranes of light, here among the chug of ghosts, where the rivers will outflow us all.

Poor Kid's Obituary

I didn't really know him but knew him too well because I too knew hurt. He lived far off Lornfield road in a trailer stained orange with rust. His were the sinewy limbs of the perpetually ground down, the worked since they could walk. Emaciated face of hunger. The strength of three kids our age, body and mind, cloaked in a shabby coat of unbreachable armor. He could outnumber the pushups and pullups of the baddest motherfucker in the whole school, and did, as if he didn't have enough to endure. Or so I remember, now, how life's cruel choirs glanced off his unbathed skin, his Salvation Army sweatpants, pushed past gashed shinbones to knees toughened and flattened by prayer, his treadless shoes those goofy Velcro numbers favored by old men nearing their ends. But what we remember can get so slippery, like the oil-slick cement where he ultimately burst and bled out. Gave his life over to blue. The way the night sometimes weeps and rain suicides itself into the street. Molecules blown apart. Seeps into the drains and the pores of the earth. Becomes vapor. Returns to the air, to our lungs, our blood. Yes, they come back again and again, invade our cells. Always inside us. After all, we too are the grease in the gears, for years have known hunger and humiliation, have heard the call and felt the pull, the push to sever. Because they *are* us, those whom we never really knew but whose ghosts we do. How they mirror the smallest light inside us, always on the cusp of winking out, and so seldom enough to reignite what's kept us going this long. The singular ember, caged in our caved and aching chests, the one that, time and again, starts to darken and go cold.

Eulogy

for Jessica

But after a while they forgot about him, and his breath failed without
anybody's noticing. He simply went under. He died. I am still alive.
— Denis Johnson, "Out on Bail"

An old friend told me of an old friend's death, asked
would I help make him remembered.
She'd sat alone at the viewing because no one had told the world
he was no longer in it.

She said, *I can't let our son think*
his father didn't matter.

So I pored over Denis Johnson, because who else could say it right?
But as I've said, he was an old friend, more a peer from schooldays,
so *maybe I'm not the best to choose*, though I'd try.

We'd gone down a similar road, I'd heard,
a road that for all its nuance is the same road
leading to the same dead end.
That I am here and he is not is no miracle, but instead
the toss and tumble of a different crapshoot.
Snake eyes versus the lucky seven.
All the strategy in the world and it's gravity that
has the final say.

I find myself here, remembering a man who was last a kid
when I knew him, and turning toward myself, as we always do,

wondering what words will be unearthed when my time finally
comes, as it will.

Is it possible not to become selfish like this in the face of mortality?
To not come up empty and silent when at last there's a need to speak?
To not collide with that old fear of being forgotten because,
even though there is evidence of your life in the scars you've left
on so many hearts, there are no words?

Because really, there never are at a time like this.

Order #52, Medium Americano

"Will there be anything else?" she asks, but I've lost myself in her skin. Outside, inattentive thirty-somethings purse their lips to sip while their kids play beneath tables, plot to unscrew the umbrellas, infinite other childhood anarchies. Shadows razor the sun, their faces through the glass twisted and misshapen. Inside, around us, the clank, clatter, hiss, the smell of fresh brewed coffee, the pregnant mother seated in the corner beside the potted palm, one hand on her future, eyes on her past. "Sir?" she says, and reels me back. I know better, but I want to tell her she reminds me of a summertime decades gone. She cuts a slice of Bundt cake, the glint of the knife a wraith dancing across her face. Her slim arms, zebra'd with scars, make me think of the ways we let light in. And darkness out. I wonder if she too has the dreams that wake her to sweat and wet sheets, the solace of the blade, if the sight of one, its sound a sustained chime through all her incarnations, is enough to call it all back — the people, places, things. The unmendable wreckage. If it seamlessly intersects her life's unspooling, zigs and zags like a suture closing up a wound, or opening one up, teeth like a zipper. It's a sort of passion, pendulum'd between love and rage, the blood that moves us too much like sap to course through our mangled veins, or too thin to ever stop flowing once the cut's been made. "That'll be right up," she says, and hands me my receipt. I fold it and the paper separates the meat between finger and thumb. There are worlds inside. The coffee is hot. It burns my tongue.

Work

We worked at the labeling plant in the industrial park way out on 45. Six bucks an hour. Good money at the time, we thought. First payday we got Shank's mom to run us to Gino's for a bottle of Jager and some smokes if we bought her a bum jug of that cheap red wine she liked. Later, Mike and his roommate got to arguing over plays on an old football game dubbed on VHS. First words then fists. Luke and I slipped out beneath the shouts, sat on the curb outside my apartment passing a pint back and forth, gin that neither one of us remembered buying. By the time it was gone, the light across the way at Mike's place had gone out, like all the rest on the street, and it was almost time to get up and get ready for work.

Reunion: Cleveland, OH

Heading down Cedar toward the city and setting sun, the sky's dichotomy, gilded jet streams, creeping violet night. Flowing below the marquee, abandoned theater, collision with electric neon glow. It would seem otherworldly reflected in a puddle, if only it had rained. Inside, perched in the corner by a stickered cigarette machine. *There*, she says, *at the bar*. At first we're perhaps just shadows, but we resolve and recognition shapes a face. Then, the ritual. Of those who once shared the same descent. Bowled over by the knowledge: some things change and some things stay the same. The show starts and the crowd gets thick. Some leather-clad cat looking straight outta *Superfly*, and this place— all its in-your-faceness. Outside after in the growing cold, he says the show was like *melted tires on the moon*, and you say, *Yeah, that's about right too, ain't it?* Seven years and we've reconvened, several hours then take our leave, the same but different. Past our normal hour, find the long way home, moon waxing beyond the glass. Muse on life's cyclical strut and cherish who we were. And who we ar

Poem Written in the Infirmary of the Old Mansfield Pen

Sunlight slicing through the slatted windows, where a small group
gathers to get a glimpse of the inmates moving across the yard of the
prison next door, as if all part of the tour. *Whatever you do, don't take
pictures*, the guide says. *They have cameras trained on you and will track
you down.* But you can see the bare desire in their eyes, for a keepsake,
imprisoning the blue streams of men further and forever in the cloud.
I could tell them I already have a picture of those stone walls, razor-
coiled gates. We are on a bus, each shackled to the man beside us, and
shackled to the floor. The driver has stopped to pick up some transfers,
joining our batch of cattle-packed bodies on the trip south, to the gavel's
judgement. Turrets needle the sky of a new season and several of us,
weary, need to use the bathroom after the dreary drive from Lorain.
They don't even offer us a jug to piss in. We aren't people anymore.
Some of us rest our heads against the bar of the seat in front of us, cold
metal pressed into our skulls as we move through rising hills and small
towns like the ones most of us were born into, where we learned, long
before this, the value of folks like us. When at last we reach the last stop,
we're herded into a long concrete stall with a single stainless-steel toilet.
We let ourselves loose in the corners, soaking one another into the soles
of our state-issued slip-ons, the smell of us sharp and piercing, our
breathing heating the room, the fluorescent bars in the ceiling washing
us into ghosts in orange clothes, the testimonies of a hundred or more
stacked up years scribed on our skin. On our faces, our dirty hands. I
could tell them this, and how some things get seared into the mind. The
only still-frame any of us would ever need.

One More While the Wind Blows

for T. L. Sherwood

So many times we've asked, *Where'd the time go?* but can only keep track by the limes in the bottom of the glass—

And maybe the next one is merely because the trudge back to the Ford on this moody afternoon, cold and white, so full of bluster and too much bite, seems a trek not to be tested, a distance these booted feet and cuffed jeans would rather not cross. Maybe it's the recessed light, Doris Day crooning from the juke, the sunken leather, the drunks in their midday haste to still the shakes. Maybe it's them not turning their heads, minding their own, keeping these secrets we hoard like riches, ones we're too afraid to spend. Maybe it's the life of a woman, singing, swinging from the silver screen. Maybe it's this booth, these empty hours between. Maybe it's a dream and just that simple.

Notes on the Irretrievable Dream

Mama taught you how to want but make do, 'cause wanting was good, like California dreamin', but dreams wouldn't feed you. Still, you tried in that way that wasn't really trying: smoking and scribbling in black-light basements to the round-and-round static sound of scratched records. Seeing and planning but never on your feet. Never socking away your pennies but trading them for the next worn-out vision. Waiting for the planets to fall in line. The soundtrack of days was deep fuzz and single-coil spank, wet as a slick pomp dragged back and piled high. Always thinking you were born too soon or too late. Playing shows in catacombs and dives and that one time, the High Five, elevated stage and smoky glow, strung limbs like a marionette's. But *this* is your time and always has been. So where'd you go, and the music? Too quick with the ethos to get a good grip. Sharing twisted takes and dull points, sharing one another's blood. Still, you won't open an umbrella in the house, or set shoes on the table, 'cause Mama taught you that was bad luck.

Dream Poem: Taos, NM

Sometime after 6am, I wake and go back to sleep. We are somewhere, you and I, a place both familiar and strange, in that dream way, and you go inside a hospital, as if to ask for directions. In a twist I'm back in that old scene: something looming, a substance on my hands I can't quite see. I can't go back and can't go on and my pockets are filled with broken glass. Then you send me a message, between these two places, crossing who knows how many borders to reach me. "It's done" is all it says, and somehow, I know you're gone. No one believes me and I can't wake up. When I finally do, the room is cold. A fly knocks against the screen.

Genovese

On the buckling sidewalk of Guadalupe, between a blond-brick church and the pulsing red of a traffic light, a woman sees a man lying still, face up and eyes closed. But it's morning, and there are cars. Surely another will stop to see if he's okay. Dogwoods line the street, shed their white and pink blossoms like the windblown crepe of paper crosses. The perennial shrine of a boy who bled out in the cold last fall. Because someone would stop. Surely someone would go to him. The congregation of stuffed bears holding vigil could be any number of those in the baby girl's crib, behind the east window on the second floor of the house with the yellow door. Below, a father listens to a monitor's oceanic static. A stirring when she turns. Tonight shots ring from two places. Through a window. From a speaker. When he moves her to the back room, where a branch scratches at the screen, he presses his face into her hair, that baby smell already fading, and listens. He doesn't pick up the phone. Though it's late, there are so many people in the neighborhood. Surely someone will do it.

Poem for the Going and Gone

Weeks before winter, the strips thin out and places where once we'd ride the night grow ghostly—the curbs and benches, the spot beside the bank, where we'd sift snipes like panned gold from ashcan trash and stitch seasons into songs. And inside we'd hide from daylight, earth's tilt turning cool to cold to colder to hurt and the sun would only rise to make us snow blind in the spiral. And to think we thought we had it beat. Whose shadows are we? We who toss away clean time like so many coins into the wish fountain. Lifelong pleas plunked and rippled, met time and time again with only an echo. But oh, the sidewalks in spring—record shops with doors propped open, rows of free-bin LPs tucked under our arms like children, sunlight folded into our pockets to warm us later, like the first burn of a single-barrel straight or the soft massage of a filling vein, a spilled glass of warm water, up the spine and across the shoulders, a weight that feels like love. The nights posted up outside the concert hall, reading aloud the names and phrases painted on the crumbling walls, where we spoke in tongues and let the night take them, carry them over the skyline, the river, the streets that were once our streets, blocks demolished and with them that time, those stone stairwells we descended with brilliance shining from our throats in golden shafts, keeping alight what would soon burn out if not for us, you and me and all the others unbound but bound for this thing that keeps calling. And who would grieve our leaving? Who would fill the space where we carried our dead? Still, some things are worth it. Known only after. A point at which it all becomes a sigh of survival or just another fissure in a heart which beats itself toward stillness, toward some kind of dark, or light.

Grand Plans

It was supposed to be the city—that huge fruit—where a friend from school was set to work backstage in the theater, tug ropes and hoist bags of sand, make worlds emerge then recede into the hushed black. But we were broke and knew what a joke it was, so it became the Ram 350 from a West Side lot, the cut check of a piece-meal loan, the loose plot, the road. Thousands of miles and a hundred songs. Cornfields, rivers, the Great Plains pooling out. Ghost shimmer of the place where plates collided and the land rose up. Slowed to settle, that small pocket where the brush burned daily, the trees, the hillsides hazed with smoke. The orchard across the road, the pump-house, the small gray boat and green water, the bank where the willow hung its head. It had been a fluke, how we lost everything and pressed on, leaving behind us dark clouds and dust.

Before the Mind and Body Fail, as Is Their Fate

after Sean Thomas Dougherty

Do not assume there is a point to any of this, except that I have tried, sought to know the question if not the answer in everything that has hurled itself against the door of me, in every image that has crashed through these twin apertures, curled itself along these optic nerves, waded in the flooded rift of synapse. In the old men who grieve over gardens and graves, who leave their lights on and doors open for their dead. The women folded like paper swans, frozen in time. The painted freights that wail all night past the last mill. In the stories stuck in the hollow bones of the city, the sirens splitting the air toward a life cut short, the bullets that bowled the body over. In the howling vacancies and reclaimed remains of East Side streets. In the rusting bridges of Cleveland and Youngstown and Pittsburgh, in the burning metal smell of a third shift along the river, the smokestacks spewing ghosts. The tombs of avenues standing slant like crooked teeth, from Judson to the overpass and deep into the valley, lots dotted with irrevocable ruin, the Isaly's diner, where boys broke fast and last night's drunk, in the market across the road, where they stole smokes and sent the songs of their boredom skyward, like bird chatter the clatter of smashed glass bottles, in the clinic where they went to kick but got kicked out, the sober club, where those that made it, clinging the wagon reins, could get a hot cup and hold each other up for an hour or two, sometimes the only difference between living and dying. In the funeral processions you can set a watch to. In the bodies of trod upon gods. And as long as this form still stirs, as long as this mind keeps at bay the small betrayals, as long as they both withstand the cage of aging, I will lean into the turning, strip every scrap of salvageable grist from this burning world, grip them in my fist, white-knuckled, and work the knots before they're lost, before at last it's all forgotten.

In Dreams

It's only ever there, in the bad ones, I dare to picture the absence of you. Not like the time you stopped breathing in the house on East Avenue when rain fell cold and flooded the gutters, when I approached the bridge of that song I wrote, looked up to see you blue, a string of spit dripping from your chin. When I was forced to find out if I could bring back the dead. Not like the time a stranger called from your phone — *There's been an accident* — and I stumbled up Mahoning trying to thumb a ride, keeping my bleary eyes peeled for your ghost, when at the hospital I followed your voice's echo through the corridors of tiled floors and too-bright light — *It huuuuuurts* — and they wouldn't give anything for the pain after getting a look at your arms. When you lay braced in the bed begging for me to go cop and we took turns in the bathroom, your frail frame saved but shaking. When we went to the impound and found what we could salvage, the kit in the console wedged between mixtapes and the engine that should have crushed you like an empty can. But your body sank into the smallest space. No, in these dreams it's the things you do that drive me mad, their lack that guts me like a rundown house, heart and every shred of feeling stripped like copper to be sold as scrap across the river. In them you're gone without a how. Always in aftermath. When I find the drawers and cupboards shut. Wrappers in the trash. Lids on tight. I'm folding laundry, hollowed, not finding shirts inside out, the way you'd always leave them. No more detritus of rushed meals crumbing cluttered counters. Just this vacancy, reminder of how you'd forget the flowers in the vase, petals shed, brittle and ungiving. Our children remain ungrown and waiting for you to come home. Myself in motion lest I drop, moving room to room, replacing all of your halted traces. Even now, awake, I see myself there, here, opening the things I forced closed. Littering every surface with you. Unrighting things thought wrong. Standing at the mantle, thinking: *What I wouldn't give to behold your withered roses.*

Gravities

A place called Skully's. 80s-night, ladies' night. Music that once grated now striking the nostalgia nerve. Enough to steer me to this rail, scrawl it on a stack of napkins to be wadded later into balls or stored in an old briefcase on the closet shelves of my cycling lives, never to be deciphered. A friend moves on the floor, serpentine through lights and synth-driven bodies, and the woman he's with, the two of them linked, skeletons eliminating space, scars kissing scars—there is scarcely greater beauty in this world. Later, she will shed her red dress and suspend herself from the ceiling, hooks pulling her pale flesh like a tent across the weight of her bones as she rises above us. And we will watch, awed, before turning back to our moored days and nights, our own small ascensions, which have yet to lift us anywhere.

2: For Love

All things
carry within
some undoing.

—Steve Lambert

Hopscotching Across this Rock

Lying in the bed's knit tangle,
slick and spent,
trying to decide what to do
come summer.

I say, *New York's too expensive.*
You say, *We could always live in the woods.*

And with no more sounds
but wordless whispers
we imitate the twisted linens
with our own hot limbs.

Northward into the thicket,
wild peninsula,
turning our backs to the Belt's
rusted husks,
using maps, not satellites.

Thunder Bay is where we cross,
Grassy Lake and on
to Riding Mountain,
with its water's cold shock,
chest-deep and so clear
we can see the clay
between our toes.

Crossing back we trade
the interstate's blue veins
for back road capillaries, taking in the bigger
picture:

Black hills and yellow grass, rolling,
rolling.

I say, *This is what it's all about – finding*
something untouched
and unmoved
to move us.

Getting drunk in the sharp shade of Devil's
Tower,
making love on the sidewalk under a dome
in Missoula
by the river,
strumming chords and banging drums on
Seattle streets, sharing wine with strangers,
amphetamines with runaways, taking the
ferry to the rim, losing control on the edge of
the world, and just too damn busy living to
write it all down.

Near Klamath Falls,
not far from the California line,

surrounded by orchards and burning hills,
we rest our engines
and stay our balding treads.

We breathe,
thinking we've found
whatever it was
we were looking for.

But as cloudless skies
give way to a darker season, the rains wash
away the surface, and we discover we've
brought ourselves with us.

On a tiny mattress
we curl into each other,
talking of that other place.

I say, *I'm so sorry I've been this way.* You say,
*I just want you to be happy. What is it I'm
trying to find?* I ask. *I don't know,* you tell
me,
only you can know for sure.

Lying in our too-small bed,
sick and spent,

trying to decide what to
do in this dead December.

Come on, you say,
let's go home.

On Being Asked What I Fear Most

I keep coming back to this:
losing love and what I might do.
But not my store of it, or that quick-spark fire
of weekend lust-love, days long burned away,
no, but the love that grinds your teeth and
makes the jaw flex, the love that makes you guilty
when you don't show enough love,
when you pick apart the little things
and forget to take a breath, to see what's right
in front of you, when you yell,
because sometimes it's the only thing that's heard,
yell do-this-don't-do-that but are real careful not to yell
Damn it, what the hell's wrong with you?
because you know words can break and buckle love.

I mean losing love's presence in unthinkable ways —
taken, cut down, removed.

This is an ugly place for all its beauty,
and no other love lost would undo me like this,
would drive me to drive through this city
as I so often do, unable to let go of my becoming, my
closing down of body and brain, fencing them in
and boarding them up like so much
of what's left standing here.

And only time would be my demolition,
wearing me down to dust, or else
some wretched chemistry
fed by my own careless hand.

Days Inn, Milwaukee

We ate burgers and beer cheese soup at the restaurant next door, a place in the midst of an identity crisis. Couldn't decide if it was a sports bar or some rustic wilderness lodge in the north woods. After, we swam in the indoor pool and I lost my ring at the blue bottom, stormed off without it when another gaggle of guests grouped in.

You appeared at the door, dripping wet, my ring pinched between your slim fingers. We drank cherry bombs until we got nostalgic, gabbed about saints and the great plans we'd make, if only we could make it. Then you got damp- eyed because liquor only ever made you happy-sad and horny. We fucked on the gaudy bedspread, rough polyester, while the TV blared a movie on HBO. We watched ourselves moving in the mirror, streaked with years of spent love, dried and cracked as the western hardpan we'd crossed years before, when we'd set out to find who knew what, and returned, yet to find it.

In the morning, we forced down weak, lukewarm coffee from Styrofoam cups and filled our pockets with whatever we could carry.

13 Years

Tradition says to give you lace,
but we've eaten curry on Easter & thumbed our noses
at the rest for so long, why start now.
It's so much give and take,
this love, but no matter the shape, its face
aged, it holds fast as an early image: your head on a pillow,
body curled in dim light, an ampersand in hot sheets.
How I watched the shadows of your bones make art.

A summer's circles overlapping,
Venn diagram of yours & mine & ours —
gathered in the park, the field beside the silver bridge,
between the mossy rocks, winding through the rows
of roses. You, working the till, & I, drunken
bookstore voyeur, spying through the spines.
Your eyes at the first scare & the uttered word of love.

The half-planned miles that would take us far & back
to a heartland city gone dark: the curbside couches
burned through, a perpetual turn from conscious
to nod, the daily replay, skipped track
of a scratched record. The prison before the slam.
The breathing metaphor.

How we reduced our lives into a life
too small for all but the smallest objects,
but big enough for love.

The decade & change spent growing, pressing walls
outward, spreading new ground, accumulating
space & what has filled it.
How we've doubled & grown old, betrayed
by our bodies, wearied by our roles and fearful
our finite time is not enough for more
than working, wearing down, wishing for sleep.

But let us keep sight of & hold tight this life we've
survived to get here, that's waited for our arrival,
for us to notice, to do our best & rest easy
in knowing that love is here even when
our eyes are closed.
And if these lines can weave a thing, keep them,
hang them like a lace curtain, watch them
billow for you
in the daylight.

Secrets, a Second Skin

We keep these parts of ourselves
to ourselves,
bone sacks hung on racks and hidden
behind locked doors.

We can't sleep,
stalked in soaked sheets, consider
what choice will be made
and wade into it,
but slow
so not to come unmoored,
to move too far from the solace of silence,
wonder what angle would change
the shape of it, this thing that knocks against
our windows and walls, bores its nails
into our soft gray matter.

We breathe deep and graze the darkened space.
But where's the edge — where does the frame begin?
How do we contain this?

Strangers

We have become a rehearsal for grief,
all our small deaths—the gulf of the mattress,
the passing as strangers in the hall, the silence
where there were words, the cessation of shared
skin—

leading to this drift,

have become a language neither one speaks, our
tongues trapped in a foreign country that once felt like
home.

Out in the yard the magnolia refuses to bloom,
the last of last year's petals dry and curled like claws,
the dogwood by the bedroom window is infested,
the lilacs keeled into the grass—you see,

even these are fading.

If this We Can Repair

It was a night like this: holed up
in a room, miles from the tethers
of our lives, secreted away, the winter
weather making the earth speak
beneath the weight of ice,
frozen fangs hanging from eaves
and jagged branches.
And how now we've escaped
to this small shelter,
to return to ourselves, rekindle the blaze
of days burned down to ash and char.

Only it was summer then, the off season
of a lakeside strip, a town of ghosts,
where at most a staggering body or two
told us we weren't alone.
The lights of the bars and countless arcades
gone dark the day the place emptied out
like an open wound.

I had such a clear vision: we would walk
to the water's edge and I would dirty my knees
in the sand while the tide lapped at your ankles,
the sun pressed flat, karat-ed in glowing gold,
the lake a rippling sheet of fire.
I would ask you for eternity and offer it back.

But in the cottage we'd borrowed,
we tarred our veins and slept

until the moon had replaced our star
and the only glow was the cop's spotlight
catching me in a half-nod, unbuckled,
pissing behind a bush.

Later you sat in a chair by the gazebo and
I knelt before you, as I might when readying your
slim, pale arm, a clumsy, stuttering attempt to
resurrect my proposal, muttered with my head
in your lap.

Here, now, the heater on high,
its rush like the ocean trapped in a shell,
could be the water that roared
all around us.

A History

The first time, you were sitting at the top of the stairs calling but I couldn't hear, so you chose the one who did. Later, you were going on the road with your old man, and you leaned out the window of his rig, stabbed me with a look I couldn't comprehend, and pulled the cord, the air horn signaling your departure. But you came back, and years later we kissed on the back porch of the house behind the bar, outside the apartment building up on High, the hill above the trailer park where I'd once lived with my mom and a slew of would-be fathers. Yours was the first tongue I tasted, but your mouth was dry as paper. And how you loved to kiss when we were young, you older than me, a woman in shape and in my mind. Your cousin was my best friend and you sent him to my house to get me. *She'll show you her titties if you kiss her for a whole minute*, he said. I would have done it anyway, but I was boy besieged by newness, so I struck the deal. There were times after, too, in the room above the beauty shop where your mom cut hair. On the couch when my mom was at work. Then there were the years to come. You became a mother, I a father, but not to each other's children. I put you in a story once and made you suffer. I'm sure you have, as I have, in the way that people who come from where we do tend to. In the story it was a time before us, a hard winter. I changed your name, hoping you wouldn't feel it.

Winter Wedding at the VFW

The bride is my mother's age
and working on number three,
a ratty man with a few good teeth,
while the hired band stands blazered
in white, a quintet of ghosts, burning
through a catalog of classics
on a make-shift stage.

Pairs of bodies part and come together,
in the coat room, outside in the chill,
where neon beer signs make embers
of the falling snow.
We swallow what we can
from flimsy plastic cups
and pay our dollar to dance,
to pretend we aren't hopelessly alone,
even if the morning finds most of us
bruised, quietly cut open.

The opening trill of "Love Me Two Times"
spills from battered amps
and fills the rented space,
while the heat of a hundred broken hearts
in need of mending moves us,
the last of the lost ones,
who would be happy enough
to be loved just once.

For Love

"Don't be afraid, mister. I won't kill you. I'm only going to take your eyes."
"But what do you want with my eyes?" I asked again.
"My girlfriend has this whim. She wants a bouquet of blue eyes. And around here they're hard to find."
— Octavio Paz

It was inching toward dusk when she said, *I've always wanted someone to bring me flowers.* From where we sat, on the drop-off overlooking the mill, watching trucks surge past along the curve of road below, where it had exiled much of the hillside neighborhood half a century ago, when the trains still ran and the black stacks still churned out smoke, I could see the chicory blossoms choking the sun-scorched berm by the thousands, pale and fluttering. A garden of light blue eyes. For the longest time, I'd wanted to put them in a poem. But I didn't say this. Or how they reminded me of a story I'd once read, about a man who almost lost his eyes, plucked like grapes from their wiry stalks, in the name of someone else's love. Instead I slid down the rocky bank, almost tumbling into the path of a growling Kenworth, and gathered them in a bunch. Air horns blared as I scrambled back. *They're beautiful,* she said, clutching the segmented stems as the diesel wind dragged her black hair sideways. *Thank you.* Did she see them as I did, as now I always would? I smiled. Wondered if she had such whims as this. The poem, I decided, was in not knowing. Whether she would ever ask for such a thing. And what I could do if she did.

3: Somewhere Else

I see you all
thoughtlessly
through a carefully inverted piece
of tainted glass

shattered in heaven
and found on these streets.

—Jim Carroll

The First Time She Died

I don't remember if it was raining,
but it was cold:
that time in late autumn
when everything's damp,
and winter has begun its cruel creep.

She had come home from work
to our place on East,
where I'd spent days awake,
struggling with words
in the company of many false shadows.

She sat on the cherry-burned couch
and shot her arm with a beautiful bullet,
leaning back
and looking loved
as the wave swept over.

After moments
that marched by like hours,
I raised my sight from a spiral-bound babble
to find her blue and breathless
with leaking lips.

Panic
— the only thing
that tied me to this world.

The sound of wood on wood as
the guitar hit the floorboards

and I forgot all the things I ever knew
and everything I never knew and
tripped over prayers to God
as I raced to the kitchen for water to
wet her face and then tried to
breathe life back into her lungs
but her jaw was locked like
so many doors—

Time stopped

for moments
that marched by
like hours . . .

But suddenly the hinge came free
and she gasped,
sucking in the stale air.

I sat her upright
on the couch where she died,
her eyes glassy and far away.

Take a sip of this,
I urged her gently
handing her the filthy glass.

She drank slowly,
and finally, a quivering question:
What happened?

Death's blue retreated,
though her flesh was still shades
too pale.

Just sit still,
I've got you.

And from there the road stretched out,
and together upon it
we would claw and tumble
while we practiced the art of
dying for a living.

Sleep

We used to joke there'd be enough
when we're dead,
postponing however we could
that nightly repose until it became
a weekly relapse of slipping under,
all those hawked hours, those midnights
and premature dawns to curtail the final sleep
while hurtling toward it, us unspooled
in streets and strange rooms,
grinning spindles glazed in salt.

Walking South down Pearl Alley

And there you were, drinking sparks
while the fumes of your past evaporated,
writhing like heat-slither on highway asphalt,
turned into one more blur you'd someday
turn away from, until you were once more
face to face, your throat on fire, eyes bled,
heart as stark as an unmarked grave,
with the only world you've ever known.

Ghost in the Root

My tooth aches,
this throb at the slightest tip
of tongue or lip must be a phantom like
the ghost of a lopped off limb, but they
burrowed down into soft pink
pulp, hollowed the root
stripped it
of each
rotten
nerve
until it was an emptiness
topped off and patched over
with man-made enamel,
buffed and polished,
still the real thing but a husk
like those years of apprehending lost rushes
and after when feelings returned
unplanned for and all at once
too much.

Pub Crawl

The bumper clipped her at the knees,
her hip the pivot the body circled,
arcing like a thrown stone
away from the grip of gravity and back,
splayed where she last staggered
into a street that devoured sound and released
silence, momentary pause of expiration
before the screams.

Springtime in Rip City

Alone and adrift in this
gray city,
the scent of dead roses
on the wind,
slick pavement stained
with slanting rain,
I drown the unknown hour
with the drones and lonely
moans of motel blues,
while the pulse of a dive
called the Alibi
flickers on the yellowed wall.
How have I landed here,
taking breaths between
clenched teeth,
waiting to return?
My lungs fill with neon light.
I feel inside my blood
the hissing streets,
the expired fire
of a thousand
vagrant stars.

The Hill

They call it The Corridor now,
but to those that live there it's still The Hill,

the avenue that runs cracked and deep,
and those who've come up here

quick to claim one end or the other:
from up the hill or down the hill,

from the blocks by Big A's and
The Foster, or the padlocked lot

that used to be a drive-thru, where
you could cop dope, liquor on Sundays,

and on the wide side streets the hustle
crowding out that brass clang and ghost

bell of a hey-day trolley, still there behind
it all, if you listen — and if you look, men

laid out in St. E's after being lit up,
convalesced and back at it. Bullet holes like

merit badges, constellations of scars.
But flipping burgers don't pay. And even the

cost of breathing seems steep, so what to do when
it's here they're kept to keep from coming up?

Here, where folks are hot to spot in the way you
talk, who's been busted and who they can trust.

Like Any Other

It's a blur of years and detox beds and concrete cells and broken oaths
and judgments.

Before that it's night and he lies curled on a stranger's couch, barely
able to keep water down, in the dark as interstate traffic paints
the dingy walls with smears of light.

Before that he Pollocks the sticky tile floors of a Wendy's single-serve
shitter with his insides.

Before that he retches in a roadside ditch at dawn while some black-
toothed hag changes a flat tire and orders him in her rusty
voice to watch for the cops.

Before that they're driving, looking for someone he doesn't know,
and he doesn't care because his body is pricked with warm
rain, his head stuffed with beautiful cotton.

Before that they climb mountains of boxes and clothes in search of a
place to worship and she gives him a bottle of pink liquid to
drink while she crushes little white pills and chokes her bony
arm with a knotted shoelace and shoots them in her wrist.

Before that it's night and she's saying, "Wanna take a ride?"

Before that he's manning the kegs at a party picked at random,

    someone asking, "Who do you know here?" and he's saying

    "Dave" because chances are there's a Dave, there's always a

    Dave.

Before that it's the humming freeway to another

city. Before that it's early on a Friday.

Before that he's bored, just bored.

Before that he's lonely kid, just like any other.

Dust & Ash

Has there ever been a time when our shoulders weren't bowed beneath a great weight, a thing pressing us into the dust that has come and will be coming? What wide spaces we scavenge, like gulls in the sand. The sky burns and here we are, pecking through shards for something to sustain us. How the dream of rain carries, etches the world, then rips it into strips when we reach out our hands. What are trees are not trees, but these upright bones and gashed knees sunk in the ashes.

The Golden Bullet

after Terrance Hayes and Gwendolyn Brooks

Knuckle-skinned   and   heart-stripped   you

slip   within the schism   and there now   are

untethered   adrift   but branded   the

mark raised fresh in a rose   of wax flesh   beautiful

what   remains   of some   half

truth   or sweet deceit   once hissed from the center of

a vacant space   where   life   was   a

flask   uncapped   tipped over   time   the golden

bullet   to kill   the hurt

A Grave Ghazal

Numb and certain it will never end,
he ignores the warnings of each one's end:

The feeling never lasts forever;
give it time and it will end.

Learns flying is a lot like drowning—
it's all the same in the end.

Soon frigid mornings stay the same,
each begins but does not end.

When uncurling from the twisted sleep,
questions, *Will it ever end?*

In a prison-bed with sheets like chains,
seems to be the road's dead end.

Bill feels ill from the stun-gun poppy,
then draws the blinds and meets his end.

Come a Long Way

From sleeping on the floor and make-shift beds
or couch cushions pushed together,
tremor-shocked bodies locked and locked out, of hope.
The self-imposed homelessness of truckstop parking lots,
tacking up tattered curtains against the agony of light.
Boosting a path across towns and counties,
waiting on the clinic to open, on the promise of a broken crutch.
Days of razorblades, hidden under scorched tongues,
of whispering wants turned into screaming needs.
Of getaways and a.m. apprehensions, handcuffs and rights
read, synchronizing alibis, and sharing backseats, shackled.
Cold stone of a holding cell, of never rolling over,
the crack of the gavel, a bell across time.
Years breathing free and even now it sounds
so clearly in your ears.

Redemption

It still boggles my mind when my daughter,
like her brother before her, sees me and smiles.
When she runs to me and reaches up to be lifted.
Who would have thought back then, every day
a thread above fire, one bad deal away from
the final takedown — by Task or bullet or maybe
a dirty batch — that I could claw my way back
here to a place where she rests her head and
breath against my shoulder, and sleeps, safe and
loved and worlds away from the man I was?

Imposter

I've come up in streets and fields,
but there's a cost to being able

to switch so quick, to belonging
everywhere and nowhere at once,

to keeping pace with laze or bustle
and finding a shield in the right stride,

to feeling like the real deal
or the fraud that wears his face.

The Body's Memory of Days Dying
after Coronavirus

If not for the constant exhaustion,
the cold-turkey likeness of it,
aches so akin to that old sickness
I can feel myself parked
on some street or in some alley,
invisible bugs crawling like electric
currents over every inch of skin,
burrowing bone deep,
waiting for that poisoned balloon,
milk of a bulb bled before it bloomed —
I could almost laugh.
A quarter million gone and counting,
more writhing behind closed doors,
masked in terror,
others unmasked, indignant
or in denial.
After all, magnified it's no more
than a cluster of berries, a pompom poof
on a child's hat.
And what a name!
As if something to stuff a lime into,
to toss back while dreaming
of sun-brushed beaches.
As if this thing surrounding us
were merely a ring of light.

Poem Written in a Walgreens Parking Lot During a Pandemic in the Rain

I drove to the next county, across abandoned tracks and past industrial ghosts to the pharmacy on West Main for my third inoculation, and parking lots like this one always conjure the spot where Pat and I would park against the curb at the back to wait for Carlos or one of the others to roll up, twenty minutes unfolded into time with no borders, our edge the concern of none but our bodies slowly then quickly slipping into sickness. And the ease of the needle into the meat of my arm, too, summons that summer, days of all seasons, all the waiting we did, to live or die, whatever came first, the leg work leading up to it, the nascent boosting, the faulty plots, the scraping together for a few balloons, never really reaching reprieve before the bled blood dried on our sleeves and it had to be fed again, the mouth of mourning that lived in our chests and the cage of our bones and guarded us from ever achieving an unblemished belief in our own light, and how it could shine brighter than the summer sun that made us into anvils hammered by its brutal heat, or the sheen of the rain-painted streets, or the snow that cloaked and made us blind as we froze by the side of the road off Sinclair by the Sunoco station in my blue Malibu with the tape deck reeling sounds from a box beneath the seat. And chances are I'm again here waiting for the chill to set in like we did daily back then, by the hour by the end of it, a moment or two of weightlessness between if luck rode shotgun, which it rarely did, so we rarely dared to make that wish.

Archives

Open eyes hope
for the single image that will capture
the last remaining sorrow,
the echo, the ghost of this city's generations
and that of the world outside,
a world gone, another going without direction,
steered by stilled hearts and veering fast,
downward, too late to save.

Shoveling Snow

Not bound for snow but by it,
thinking about AA and all those sayings,
and those people that always have to add
who I choose to call Jesus Christ
at the end of *a God of my understanding*,
lest they be mistaken for a heathen
like the rest of us.
How once in a while they like to bust out
the old *It's the journey not the destination*.
Meanwhile their understanding is built upon
getting somewhere, their entire lives lived
in base desire to reach those golden streets.

I think of the monk who told his pupil:
Before enlightenment,
chop wood and carry water;
after enlightenment,
chop wood and carry water
—all while sitting among his scrolls,
not chopping or carrying a goddamn thing.

But what's the point here, anyhow?
Surely something about being present,
mindful, seeing meaning in even the most
menial labor, fortitude, accepting that one's work
is never done, et cetera.
Or perhaps it's that even fools and frauds

can pass down pearls
to turn over in the light before this window,
before the fresh white beyond
gets cleared away,
because every destination is a point of leaving,
and sooner or later
we'll need to leave this place.

Somewhere Else
for Victor

A bar with a name like that,
is it any wonder we ended
the night going too fast, you chasing
distant taillights in your two-toned
Toyota while I hung out
the passenger side antagonizing
the stars and pitching empties
to the wind, the crest and blind curve
that put us slant and dented in a ditch
beside a lake?

My seams were hooked
by brambles and left in tatters
while you phoned your brother
who knew a guy with a truck and chain.
Get outta here, you said. *My folks already
hate you.* So I walked the potted asphalt
of the no-name country two-lane,
my inner compass thrown into an unruly orbit
from eating handfuls of colorful chemicals,
toward a line of trees materializing
like ghosts in the lightening sky.

Two dogs came around a shamble shack
with lowered heads and high hackles,
another crept out of the corn, circling
until they stood flank to flank, three-headed
and hungry with a singular body, as if to
prevent my leaving this distorted dawn

I'd been lost in. And is it any wonder I'd given
myself to myth like this, a car rolled and broken,
a parting of ways, a roaming through the
gloaming of an unfamiliar wilderness?

My sandals slapped the road as it dipped
into a shadowed valley, the clacking skitter
of nails on stone at my back, until
one moment I lifted,
left the ground, body too far ahead
of feet, a failed flight, a tumble, a scramble to outrun
the gnashing teeth.
When I came to a highway
I turned toward the sun's rising
and came to rest against a gas station payphone
while trucks rumbled and spit black smoke
down the road that led, I realized then, into Pennsylvania,
Chippewa Falls, the tunnel that opens on three-river city.

I woke in bed, having dreamed I'd dreamt it,
but my keys were missing, until I made my way
back there, to that state line, found them
poking from a crack in the ground
where I'd stopped to lay my head.

4: Minutiae

Time our subtle poison runs toward us,
and through us, and out the other side.

—Jim Harrison

Aubade in the Desert

The morning is so silent here.
6am and not a bird yet singing, but a lone cricket.
The scrub stretches from the open window up the foothills
into the mountains, and behind them,
    the sun.
Perhaps this is that moment to dwell on death as so many
dead poets have, in a room haunted by
    more than one scribbling hand.
How this border time between night and day evokes
    crossing over or moving through some veil,
    impermeable at any other hour, how the lack of frenzy
    and distraction breeds fear when left alone with your
    own mortality, stone-heavy, with the clock's hands
    circling, time barreling down.
But the sun has finally broken beyond the adobe wall, spills
itself golden across the dry ground. So perhaps mortality can
wait, thoughts instead on life, moving into the next hour,
into the
    world, leaving the ghosts with the curtains parted,
    to scribble their lines in the room facing east.
Or inviting them along for something new.

Sonnet for Spring, Dead on Arrival

You're little more than a poor transition,
All dolled-up and sandwiched between extremes,
Pulled from winter's bitter indecision
With a riot of blurring births that scream
While fast wilting toward the torrid summer.
Again and again, the tilt calls you back
To the same small stretch of short-lived wonder,
Where your shades contend with the ray's impact;
But from their southern turn they burn you down,
Skip you ahead too soon with every spin,
A transient gathered, run out of town,
Made to move on before settling in,
And whose yearly epitaph will be drawn
In dirt-brown patches on yellowing lawns.

Sometime Before Dawn at the Cabin in the Woods

> *. . . and all the uncaring*
> *Intricate rented world begins to rouse.*
> —Philip Larkin

I come awake inches from the ceiling
     in an unfamiliar dark
and seek the ladder's rungs
     with bare feet black with grit.
Outside, no sound but the last rain
     weeping through the trees and laurel,
Earth's pent-up breath releasing.
     I tell myself to stay awake,
take this gift of human silence,
     make with it something
unattainable any other time,
     or simply sit a while inside it,
do nothing before the walls fall
     and the world rushes in.

Ideas

What better conceit than this
goddamn gnat zipping
in and out of the window light
at an indeterminable depth
of vision?

The nearly unseen speck in air,
there then gone, over and over,
until it fulfills some lesser or greater
fate:

erratic flight exiled to the borders
of my eyes, restless departure toward
some other rotting fruit, or finally
trapped like a paged phrase
between my clapped hands.

Year's End

Lips parted,
the open wound
of a perpetual
sigh

Minutiae

Beyond the wire fence
a rooster crows while,
above the sandy mountain
a small plane scissors the blue
toward some southern call,
gaining distance in its retreat
and leaving silence, a fading
white trail swallowed by sky,
and the music of the juniper,
drum brush swept across a snare,
the wind eddied prayer of slanted
grass in sway, thrumming of the
hummingbird, that blur of urgency,
in need and ever feeding.
Out there, there are wars without
end, mouths that will never utter
their final farewell, throats that will no
longer sing or sigh. Here, the sun
traces sharp shadows in the yard.
Beside me, a single iris blooms.

Death in the Courtyard of the House Where Dennis Hopper Lived

There's a field of stones,
each step an almost rolled ankle
or broken neck.
Hundred-year trees, tall and hacked.
Tower of the bird hotel.
A chatter from the grass,
black sheen of a many-winged chorus
gathered around its dead.
The silent bell nesting in the west wall waits
for a wind or warning.
All these doors and squares of light.
All of it here.
None of it forever.

5: Of the Season

The world that was meant to embrace us
decayed without end
and the effects of causes raged over it.

—Wislawa Szymborska

Mama

She always had to have a man, or what looked like a man, sharp arms and jaw of a man, to sit home manning up the place, while she ground down her joints into powder like we were always taught a *man* was s'posed to. She didn't mind a lowly no-account long as she knew he was there to protect her baby, keep him safe while she did what she had to do in a stretched-out nine-to-five that bled mornings into nights and jittery dawns. A man who had some link to the world, a lineage, perhaps just a drink with the right smile, someone to take and raise her baby should she crumble. There was nothing she wouldn't endure to ensure her baby wasn't left alone in some cold rental, above the bar or in that tacked-on shack with the bricks and bare board walls. She'd bear the weight of a thousand *I dos*, a thousand false rings, a thousand ruined hearts. She'd do it all in stride while her feet grew blistered, her skin loose and leeched of life. She'd be a shield in all the ways she could, waking in the dark, taking buses, stop-and-go but never not going. She had her baby to think of. She would take what came and get what didn't. She'd find a man but never to do what needed done. A man was simply a last-ditch net to catch her baby, if she happened to lose her feet out there, and couldn't keep on.

Tell Me Again, that Story

It's somewhere in middle Missouri, or maybe the vast flat of Kansas, that she tells me of the time Bobby Kennedy died. All these parts of her life she's already shared, but I ask her to share again because space like this makes you feel small, invariably aware of how little time you may have left in this life to listen.

She was eighteen and they'd driven to Steven's Point because her boyfriend was in a band, the same boyfriend that fell asleep at the wheel one time as she slept in the seat beside him, turning his Chevelle into an accordion, her head hitting the dash and gashed open. But this was not that time.

It was dawn when she woke to that liminal gray of a day not yet, but being born, still rumbling back toward home in the blooming blue, and that's when she heard the news and Marilee Rush singing "Angel of the Morning" on the radio. She cried, she says, a cry she hadn't known was welled and waiting to weep free. Even now, her eyes are wet as she tells it.

My Thwarted Abduction

I don't remember it, but once when I was still a baby, my old man tried to take me from my mother outside a McDonald's on Milwaukee's East Side. Any time we pass it, she points and says, as if for the first time, *That's where your dad tried to steal you away.*

She says two fat ladies came out of the restaurant when they saw her huddled on the pavement, holding me tight to her chest as he grabbed for me. *They chased him off,* she says, and I've tried so many times to picture it. Him fleeing, yelling over his broad shoulder and shaking his balled fist. The large women guarding her as she guarded me, no longer a small child but more like the idea of something, as though each of their fates rested on it.

This time I imagine my baby self stretched like a strand of taffy, them standing in the draft of a city bus with what's left just a mess in their hands. In another version I'm a doll made of yarn, undone loop by loop until there's nothing but knotted fingers and a formless tangle on the street between them.

Swing Shifts and Doubles

Ma was the one
who took me on the cold dark nights
and colder, darker mornings.
After all, who else was there?

Set me up in a different place
depending the time of day:
a bunk made of sacked potatoes and extra towels,
or in the boss's office with the small TV,
as many of those fountain as Cokes I could drink,
because she was one to work those swing shifts
and pull those doubles, and her boss was a decent man
who suffered kids in the kitchen.
After all, where else was there?

It got to be that place stayed with her,
the greasy spots, the splash back
from chopping and flipping on the flat top,
soaked through her apron until her own clothes
wore them like memories, ones that only grow clearer
when everything around them fades.
And she'd wear them out before herself,
before her hips and back betrayed her.
After all, what else was there?

Residual

This tattered perch tames
what was once a restless spring,
while plumbed are the depths
of memory.

A child's shaggy hair,
tangled back in the freeway breeze
as he tangles toward the unfamiliar:
tilted houses on dead end streets
and blurring rest-stop vacancies.

And now,
in this autumn,
as days gone still
still echo on the wall,
such remnants of the here and gone
reach out,
search for purchase in the space between

a latchkey kid
and part-time reverie.

That Night I Left Work with a Pocketful of Cash on Fire

and you went and fucked it up by taking a bullet
through your hand. You never watched
After School Specials, so never learned
not to do stupid shit. None of us did.
He's in the ER, Juanita said, her voice
so flat and put-out, as if describing how the dog
had just pissed all over the rug again.

You'd been playing around with it,
.25 with the pearl grip and nickel finish,
lifted by some kid from the projects
from his grandma's top drawer,
the way we did, passing it back and forth
in the lot by the tracks, killing time between
fathers and griefs.

You could still roll a damn fine joint
with your good hand bandaged,
its fingernails caked with dirt, the raw
and ragged hole, the rotten smell of it
like a body bloating in the sun, and after,
with the bones of your metacarpus
tenting upward, a miniature volcano
pressing against the puckered flesh.

It would never heal right, no feeling
but the dulling of dead tissue, the ghost

of the round ripping through it. It pulsed
with heat, you'd said of the night it had gone
off, like a glowing coal or a white-hot wire
stitched along your lifeline.

When the others came, later, penetrated
your breastplate with hot steel and black powder,
I imagined the birth of stars, a whole cosmos
swirling in your sternum. The Y-shaped incision
a question, a constellation.

On the Run, Returning

A few months back, I caught your goateed grin while thumbing through the "People You May Know" list on Facebook, a reality decades distant from our fragile, long-haired skulls in that time when we knew each other best. I'd searched for you before, in those moments after some match-flare of memory lit up the chambers of my brain, but I could never spell your last name, all those mid-syllable vowels, where to place them. Hell, we rarely called each other by our names, anyway, other than the ones we gave each other. Our handles, we called them, like we were truck drivers, like our dads, or the other men who growled through our lives, downshifting but never sticking around. You were Dirt and called me Killer because I wore a thick chain. We even had that elaborate handshake, remember?

Before I stumbled across you online, my ma had given me a clipping from the newspaper. Turned out you were you were doing a bit down in a southern Ohio penitentiary, where I'd done a little stretch myself several years after the last time I saw you. Assault, the paper said, and I remembered how impulsive you were, the both of us, all of us back then. Always looking for something to prove, an excuse to make a scene. Staring at your mugshot, I couldn't say I couldn't see it coming.

***

We are thirteen and fifteen and looking for our way

back. But this is not where it starts.

100

It starts in a house that will one day be razed, on Logan and Dennick, across from the burned-out mill.

Dude's name is Dude, and I'm talking in a time before the Big Lebowski. He's siphoned cable and juice from the house next door. All the rooms are cracked plaster, rotten wood, bare wires. Dead things in the walls.

He has a white-and-black cat named Wild Child that lives in his Chrysler and suns itself on the dusty dash when we drive out in the country on summer days, smoking joints and chugging warm beer. . . all those sins and all those wishes out there, just floating.

***

"You went ghost on me, brother." That's the first thing you say to me after all these years. You bailed me out of County in May of '99, or maybe it was June. Probably thought I've been dodging you because of the hundred-dollar bond. Not even sure what possessed me to call you that night, of all people, what made me think you'd have the scratch to come through. But you came through. Afterward, I crashed on the nasty couch on your parents' front porch to sleep off a mean mixture. You dragged my frayed ass to court the next morning, where I stood, still drunk and sleeveless in front of the judge. Then you dropped me at my ma's work and I never saw you again. But I knew I owed you. Money. Maybe something else.

***

A downtown alley between the Burger King and the New Music Station, which will become an Irish dive, then a husk and then a lot and then — what else will be left when the decades recede?

Some sort of ruin. Seeded with grass.

We breathe deep and ride our first numbing rails into the high hammering glare of a grocery store. A stolen can of nacho cheese and a bag of chips. A scatter- shot departure as the guard gives chase.

We find each other in the bushes by the bank, creep through backyards and over fences, each shadowed step leading us farther from where we need to be.

A flicked thumb. A ride.

"Where to?"

"That way, I think."

Now we're near the river, the towering past of cold stacks pressed against the night. There's the county joint we'll someday know so well. There's the bus station that will someday be both an escape and inevitable return. We're from the sticks but in the city, underage and on the run. Everything we've dreamed but never thought through.

Downtown now. How did we get this far?

***

102

I'm on my way to the walk-in clinic to see about this cough that's been wracking me since Christmas, when I stop at a red light only a couple blocks from where we fled the grocery store all those years ago, and when I look over to where they're putting up a new Rally's burger place, I'll be damned if that's not you right there beside that ditch, hooded and zipped up in a pair of faded blue coveralls, handing a piece of pipe to some guy in the trench.

The sky is the color of a dirty dishrag, and the cold air turns your breath to smoke.

There's that flare again. Those early days. Those moments that haven't left me.

Over the years, I've driven past your parents' house. I do stuff like that sometimes, because no matter how unlikely, I fear forgetting more than almost anything. One day the house was just gone. Just a big vacant space now. A couple gravel driveways and patches of high dead grass. Perhaps it's strange, but the first time I saw that emptiness, I saw in it your mother — her warm face, her milky, crooked eye — and how she used to fix us food when we came in from the cold, sprinkling tortillas with water and scorching them on the stove while we sat at the table. I smelled the meat and the spices and the smoke from her cigarette — she smoked Slim Price, I remember — and the ever-present eggy scent of well water coming from the kitchen sink. I saw the mountains of clothes everywhere. I saw your old man's chicken coop and the time you threw the grate from the grill like a Frisbee, beheading one of his fattest hens, its body running off into the brush. I saw, about twelve feet up, the room with the mattress on the floor, and the porch roof where we'd jack off side by side to ratty, hand-me-down skin mags (we never did know what it was like to have anything new, did we?). The sound of trains hid us as much as the night did.

The summer stars stared down but did not judge us.

***

We catch another ride, and another.

"We can't pay you. All we got's this knife, and we need it for

protection." "And all I got's this gun. Hop in."

We end up on Dewy, near the rehab clinic I won't know for another few years. Then again much later.

"This is as far as I'm ridin'. Good luck, boys."

Our last refuge is the neon beacon of the Adult Book on Market.

We hang among the flesh and rubber and smoke a joint with a drummer named Tim. He has a handlebar mustache and wears a gold chain around his neck, keeps nodding like he's answering a question no one asked.

At first light he drives us to your cousin Juan's trailer.

Juan lets us rest while he lifts weights and practices his boxing combos in front of the mirror above the TV, then he gives us a lift back to where our mothers are pissed off and waiting.

They've been worried sick, they say.

We glance at each other, a shared thought between us: *If you only knew.* But neither of us says it.

***

On that first contact a couple months ago, after you got out, it was all *How you been? How's your ma? Sorry to hear about your folks, man, wish I coulda been there to say goodbye. Remember that one time? Crazy days, brother, crazy days.* We made loose plans to get together soon, which is the typical thing to do, but I've got this life now, ya know, the kids and all. I still owe you, I know, and want to pay that debt. Hell, I'm sure you could use the money. I consider honking the horn, or rolling down the window and shouting your name. To let you know I haven't forgotten, any of it. But the light just turned green.

As I Lay Her Down to Sleep

Lying on my side with my back against the wall, pink paint and stickers curling like leaves, I wait for my daughter to slip into sleep, that cycle that will lead her to dreams. But her eyes are wide open beside me and the window's gray dusk. My arm is at a numbing angle, shoulder socket sore from feigning slumber. The fan rattles and whirs. I wonder what she sees during these times, what shapes in the shadows, what alien landscape she finds herself in, mountainous and half-resolved in the cracked door's slice of light. She turns and turns, reaches over to pat my face and tug my ear, assure herself I'm here. Something safe and familiar to grab hold of, to cling to as the rain riddles the roof above her bed, and the clouds growl and the sky grows darker. I'm here, baby girl. I'm right here.

Architect of Light

It's Christmastime, and my daughter hands me
colorful blocks, eyes expectant, says,
Build me something?
But what could I build to rival the bird
she held only moments ago, tall and pink
and snapped together like a flamingo she's
never seen but her fine motor fingers shaped
just the same?
Perhaps a box to house all she'll someday lose.
I'll need more blocks, I think. She runs off,
as if to oblige my mind, comes back
with a plastic bucket brimming, and as I set
to work, constructing this transient tomb
that will be dismantled long before she ever
knows love as something that can cut,
that can hurt her heart in ways that always
feel like the first, she ambles away again,
to play with a strand of battery powered
bulbs draped across the table.
She returns again, something aglow hidden
behind her back.
What you got there, sweetheart?
She smiles the smile of the never-been-broken,
reaches out,
and hands me a cupful of light.

Spies

When we were young, there were no dances or Friday night football games. By the time we had wheels, we had better things to do, laws to break elsewhere. And in the days before, our moms worked late, and our daddies were gone. They, too, had better things to do. When there was money, we came up in bars, cut teeth on pinballs and pool cues and the dregs of snuck bottles and simmering violence. On the nights when the work was done, the money all drunk, we watched midnight movies then dressed in black, left our moms to fill their ashtrays at the kitchen table, alone, the radio playing those sad songs. We'd slip into the night, gather in shadows outside windows, watch. We called it spying, this prepubescent voyeurism, and wagered what we'd see through the glass. Murder. Depravity. Mad scientists building bodies, witches stirring strange brews. But behind each pane it was just people, in chairs, filling ashtrays, and low music and the dark.

Survival Skill

My son refuses to learn
how to tie his shoes, content to move
through a life of Velcro and elastic.
My assurances that it's a valuable skill
with much carry over
cannot break past the barriers
of the worlds he's built.
If only I could convince him:
we all have this thing we cling to,
this rope,
and the tighter we tie it,
the better our chances of holding on.

This, Our Mountain

Through the grueling pace of minimum wage,
we can't retrieve meaning,
unseen from the hand-to-mouth toil
beneath the eye of a broken machine,
one that would have us believe
our lots are self-imposed,
as if we, too, have kept the collector
cuffed and closeted,
and no number of coins deposited
will soften the day's hard edge,
offer reprieve before it's all foreclosed.
And as our children are suckled on aching bones,
blind to the trials and wills that have buckled,
to the crooked backs and scarred shoulders, of
fathers and mothers pushing their boulders
up and up, again and again,
we pray they will remain
strangers to futility,
that someday
their stones
will bear
fruit.

Ode: In Utero

You, my budding unborn,
the books compare
to fruit—from seed to berry
to grape to plum—
and I can't help but find it
fitting.

Yet you were more,
the moment I saw
where your thoughts
would someday bloom,
when I took in your
flicker that quickens
each day,
and my own
slowed
then sped off
across the room, when you
unhooked me from trivial things,
shook me loose
from the mundane motions.

And now as I fumble
with feelings between two poles,
unsteady and amazed
by the gravity of something so
small,
your form takes shape,
branching out in its
amniotic cocoon,
and through your stages

111

you straighten my gait from
its clumsy stagger,
showing me there's
grace to be found
in fear

and at least one star
when the world
goes dark.

Pavor Nocturnus

1986:

She always visits in the flashes of light when it rains. Tall and but an
outline against the storm-streaked glass. A mosaic of black ants on
the wall beside her, skittering specks that change their geometry with
each fork-tongued flicker. She draws nearer. I'm just four, frozen in
the ways of dreams or fear. She has no face and does not speak. Only
raises a draped arm, reaching out, to help or hurt. Or be helped. I
can't tell which.

2004:

Was she the one who now takes to the corners   the one who
multiples the shadows of this crystalline vision   the one with whom
the bugs conspire in a wicked calligraphy on the walls and floors and
the borders of doors she must be the shade of tomorrow, yesterday
                patron saint of my layaway psychosis   is that what
keeps the pen moving and the bed so cold, in this year of no sleep?

2017:

So long it's been. So why then, now?

Perhaps a man has no control over what he remembers and forgets.
Perhaps such recollections are communicable, passed along the helix of
        our broken cells.

113

Perhaps when my son, turning four, whispers in the dark, when I find
      him reaching into empty

        air where the light casts a slant shaft into the white slit of
        his sleeping eyes, he is being helped or helping.
Perhaps the designs he traces with such intuitive grace are the
        messages I never could decipher.
        Of the ants on the wall. The shape that loomed above me.

But that's not it. Anymore. This sweet slumbering. Because now he
wakes each night screaming, eyes wide with incomprehensible fear,
looking past me, moving away, mouth rounded by inarticulate
vowels.

Perhaps I've been wrong.
Perhaps he pleads.

An Armor

after Parkland, FL

Kids aren't dying again, they're still dying,
   and the threads and diversions . . .
      have me so — tired.

My boy has a fractured leg, a moment of play cut short.
I wish I could tell him it was the last time he'll feel hurt and broken
and mean it,
   that life won't continue to steal the ground beneath him, as it
     does, to bear down.

But we tell so many lies already.

His cast *is like an armor*, he says, because it's hard as stone.
I Sharpie'd a lightning bolt down the side, and now he thinks he's a
superhero, bulletproof, invincible.

Kids are dying, dead,

dying. My kids are alive.
For now.
Shielded only by youth's fragile illusions and these four walls.

Yet what do I do but escape to this trap of mind
   to write these — what, these *poems*?

As if reflection changes facts, softens truths, makes bearable.

As if without intervention, he really could
      save the world,
           stop the bullets when they start to fly.

This Heart

The walls have collapsed,
two hands pressed together in what looks
like prayer, or an attempt to capture what
light is left from leaking, seeping
into the strange terrain of my body, or maybe
it's crushing like a closed fist what little life
is tucked inside, like a bug or a dream
that never stood a chance at all.

Bayer 81

A sharp sting in the tip of my fourth toe sent me hobbling into the walk-in clinic on my day off. But before the NP got started fingering the joint at the ball of my foot, she checked my pulse and pressure a third time. My systolic digits were on the rooftop somewhere, aimed at the apex of the sky. She began talking EKGs and ERs, said the da-dum thump of my ticker was in rhythm, not a single hitch or stutter, but the number on the pump was way to close to the edge to not fear my stroking out on the table. *You're a mess*, she said. *So what's the deal?* I told her stress but spared the rest—the abrupt but severe tumble from the proverbial wagon, the dropped reins flapping and dragging in the dust, the horses gone heedlessly off the cliff, the months digging for their bones among the rocks. *I mighta picked up some coffin nails again, too,* I said. She told me what she claimed she'd told her mother when she lost her first lung: *Masturbate instead. It's much better for you.* Then she referred me to a podiatrist and out by the water cooler tossed me two boxes of low-dose aspirin. *Keep an eye on those numbers. If they stay where they are, get to the hospital before you drop dead.* So I've thinned my blood and rubbed one out, but seated at the kitchen table still can't help but flout orders that would do me some good. I exhale, take another puff as the cuff tightens. As my throat burns and the numbers keep climbing higher.

Prison of Blood and Bone

What choice do we have but give in
and go where the body takes us?

From the start, it's a rise upward,
then slow mounting pains of nerve

and junction, torn fibers that tether us
together like dangling dolls, an alliance

with the mind, then subtle betrayals,
one moment leading the charge and

the next a quick shift into immobility,
our honeycombed bones and what they

can withstand weakened, the loads and
stresses of the physical world, the slightest

turn or bend, the unbraced for, placing it
on a horizon, that timeless axis of the dead.

Messengers

Always this labor to keep my chemicals in flow, their complex orchestra ringing at just the right frequency, to move through the day at the perfect altitude. What the brain won't do, and the meds don't steady, I supplement with things from earth and lab alike, and it's like this:

Wake. Arousal. Mind and body in tandem. Stress response stacked upon sub- optimal slumber. Caffeine subdues, barricades receptors, drills through inertia . . . Feel yourself out. Proceed from there, always with caution, braced for every potential. Mornings that hold more light disarm, as much, if not more, than the persistent, inexplicable dark. Pills are clocks that turn you toward time passed, toward the trigger and release. Electrical impulse. Transmission of feeling. Brain cascade. Synaptic deluge. And this is only morning. And most days they work but don't work. Still blockages in there. But there's a pill for that.

It's funny how they can know so much and still know nothing.

Is it any wonder why I wonder if I've doomed my children to these same shades of night and day by way of my own genetic glitch which has writ itself into their coding?

Our Church Was the Night

We were the free-lunch kids, but even then we knew wasn't anything for free, for the cost was the chorus of cash fanning out in suburban kids' hands. Kids who lived in houses and had moms and dads that were still together, who never wore anything from the church charity drive, never knew words like layaway or food stamps or clearance sale except to mold them into weapons against us. We feigned our unshakable natures, balled up the incoming fire in our fists for heat as we spent nights roaming like the strays they imagined us to be, in woods and streets, feet making tracks through back yards, wearing bare the grass behind the Dairy Mart, sowing the dirt with butts of stolen cigarettes and broken glass we passed around as if in communion with something we couldn't see but through years of repetition knew was there, the way some folks believe in gods. Our promised land too awaited: bone breaking labor, treatment centers, psych wards. Prisons. Morgues. So it was scrawled on the restroom walls. Some of us would take it and make it through, while others dissolved through the revolving door. And the truth is, we never would know which ones we were.

Of the Season

I'd like to believe
I haven't yet reached the
middle, if not surpassed
the first half, of this life.
That despite my body's slow decline,
the best is still forthcoming.
But for all the healthy choices —
the vitamins, the exertion,
sustained motion — the narrowing
spaces in my spine insist
it's only a matter of time.

A finite resource.
No matter how we divvy it up.

Years ago, I wrote of the existential
autumn, how my time was of the season,
and at times I smile at the thought of
thinking the best days were over,
that the worst to come could come
close to what I've survived.

A silly notion, that.

Yet the smile uncurls each time,
as the leaves have long since turned
toward burning and begun to fall.

The road is littered with the
dead, and winter is just around
the bend.

Notes

1. The epigraph for section 1 is borrowed from the poem "Poem Written in the Margin of an Eclipse" in Sean Thomas Dougherty's book *Scything Grace*.

2. The title of the poem "a halottak nyelve" is in Hungarian, meaning "Language of the Dead."

3. In the poem "Poor Kid's Obituary," the line "rain suicides itself into the street" was inspired by a similar line in Richard Lange's novel *This Wicked World*, which reads: "The rain came down harder, the drops slamming into the pavement like suicides."

4. The epigraph for the poem "Eulogy" is borrowed from the short story "Out on Bail" in Denis Johnson's collection *Jesus' Son*.

5. In the poem "Reunion: Cleveland, OH," the show was a small, intimate performance by the English, genre-bending band Swervedriver, whose melodic, spacey, effect-laced music never broke into the mainstream. They were and continue to be one of the most underrated and underappreciated bands from the "alternative" music scene. I recommend their albums *Mezcal Head* and *Ejector Seat Reservation* for the uninitiated, though they are all time well spent.

6. The poem "Poem Written in the Infirmary of the Old Mansfield Pen" refers to the old Ohio State Reformatory in Mansfield, OH, which was shut down in December of 1990 because of overcrowding and inhumane conditions. The replacement facility, Mansfield Correctional Institution (MANCI), stands next door to the old prison, which is currently open to public tours and was made famous for being the filming location of the motion picture *The Shawshank Redemption*, as well as

being the setting for numerous music videos and other films and tele-vision programs over the years.

7. The poem "Genovese" is a scenario based on what has become known in social psychology as "Genovese Syndrome" or the "Bystander Effect," which refers to the diffusion of responsibility that occurs when individuals who are part of a large group of witnesses do not act or call for help because they are convinced someone else in the group will or already has. This can be traced back to the murder of Kitty Genovese of Queens, NY on March 16, 1964, during which an alleged 38 witnesses saw or heard the attack but did nothing. This statistic has been proven inaccurate and the result of sloppy journalism, but nevertheless, the Genovese case led to important research in the field of social psychology and is used as a primer of this phenomena in nearly every introductory psychology textbook to date.

8. The epigraph for section 2 is borrowed from the poem "We're Killers, the Living" in Steve Lambert's book *The Shamble*.

9. The epigraph for the poem "For Love" is borrowed from the short story "The Blue Bouquet" by Octavio Paz.

10. The epigraph for section 3 is borrowed from the poem "Maybe I'm Amazed" in Jim Carroll's book *Living at the Movies*.

11. The poem "Springtime in Rip City" refers to one of several nicknames of Portland, OR.

12. The poem "The Golden Bullet" is a play on the golden shovel form invented by the poet Terrance Hayes, in which the last word of each line corresponds with a word borrowed from a line or stanza in another poet's work. Hayes used the Gwendolyn Brooks poem "We Real

Cool," so I thought it only appropriate to also use a line from a Brooks poem, the title of which is "To Be in Love."

13. A ghazal (pronounced "guzzle') is an ancient Arabic poetic form which uses a minimum of 5 couplets, each of which should be able to stand on its own as a small poem. The couplets typically end with the same word or phrase as the others, and the first line of the last couplet includes the name of the poet writing the piece. A ghazal is tradition-ally a poem of longing, and while I attempted to stick to the criteria of the form, one might argue I took some liberties in this regard.

14. The poem "Somewhere Else" contains a vague allusion to Cerberus of Greek mythology, a multiheaded hellhound that guards the gates of Hades and is tasked with preventing the dead from escaping the underworld.

15. The epigraph for section 4 is borrowed from the poem "Time" in Jim Harrison's book *In Search of Small Gods*.

16. The epigraph for the poem "Sometime Before Dawn at the Cabin in the Woods" is borrowed from the poem "Aubade" by Philip Larkin.

17. The poem "Death in the Courtyard of the House Where Dennis Hop-per Lived" refers to the Mabel Dodge Luhan House in Taos, NM, a Pueblo style structure which was built in 1800. Its namesake would go on to turn the property into an artist's colony in the early 1900s, where artists such as Willa Cather, D.H. Lawrence, Georgia O'Keefe, and others would stay and create. The actor/director Denis Hopper discovered the place while shooting the film *Easy Rider* and purchased and lived on the property through most of the 70s. It is currently used as a retreat/conference center.

18. The epigraph for section 5 is borrowed from the poem "One Version of Events" in the great Polish poet Wislawa Szymborska's book *The End and the Beginning*.

19. The poem "This, Our Mountain" makes a not-so-subtle allusion to the story of Sisyphus in Greek mythology, whose crime, which led to his pushing a boulder up a mountain for eternity, was that he tricked Thanatos (Death) when he came for him and chained Thanatos up instead when he demonstrated how the shackles worked. With Death imprisoned, no one on Earth could die. Once Sisyphus was caught, he was given the punishment we all know so well.

20. The phrase Pavor Nocturnus is Latin and refers to a specific sleep disturbance or "parasomnia" known as a "night terror," typically experienced in early childhood and decreasing in frequency with age. During a night terror, which usually occurs during the first hours of non-REM sleep, the sufferer appears to be having a nightmare while awake, experiencing extreme arousal in the form of panic, disorientation, elevated heart rate, even hallucinations. The episode can last anywhere from 1-10 minutes, and the sufferer typically has no recollection of the event the next day.

21. The poem "An Armor" was my first and only written response to the continual, unresolved crisis of mass shootings in our country.

About the Author

William R. Soldan is a fiction writer and poet from the Ohio Rust Belt and the author of five books across genre, among them the linked story collection *In Just the Right Light*, the poetry collection *So Fast, So Close*, and most recently, the novel *Undone Valley*. Published widely in print and online venues, his work has been nominated for the Pushcart Prize multiple times, Best of the Net, Best Small Fictions, a Derringer award, and has been included in and received honorable mention in *The Best American Mystery Stories* (2017/2018). He currently lives in Youngstown with his wife and their two children. He's a high school drop out with a BA in English Literature from YSU and an MFA in Creative Writing from the Northeast Ohio Master of Fine Arts program. His former jobs include cook, bartender, bouncer, factory machinist, personal trainer, college writing instructor, and a host of other things. Currently, he works as a maintenance man for a non- profit community center. He can be found @RustWriter1 on the Twit box for those looking to connect.

www.ingramcontent.com/pod-product-compliance
Lightning Source LLC
Chambersburg PA
CBHW030313130626
46549CB00002B/829